THE NIGHT BEFORE SERIES™

# The Night Before Francis Wrote a New Song

Written by: Timothy Penland
Illustrated by: Kayee Au

canecreekpublishers

dawson media®

'Twas the night before Francis
Wrote a new song
A battle was raging
It was fought all night long.

It was 18 and 14
The nation at war
With England again
Just like before.

The site was a fort
McHenry by name
The British were outside
Bombarding the same.

The fort was located
In Baltimore town
With warships determined
To knock its walls down.

The shelling was heavy
With no end in sight
Francis Scott Key
Watched it all night.

He was on board a ship
One attacking the fort
The next day he planned
To return to the port.

He had boarded the vessel
Seeking a friend
A prisoner named Beanes
A man he'd defend.

He was told to stay put
Though he'd won Beane's release
So he stayed on the ship
'til the firing had ceased.

As he stared in the night
The shelling was strong
The fort took a beating
The night seemed so long.

He just couldn't see
How the fort could hold out
He feared for his own life
His future in doubt.

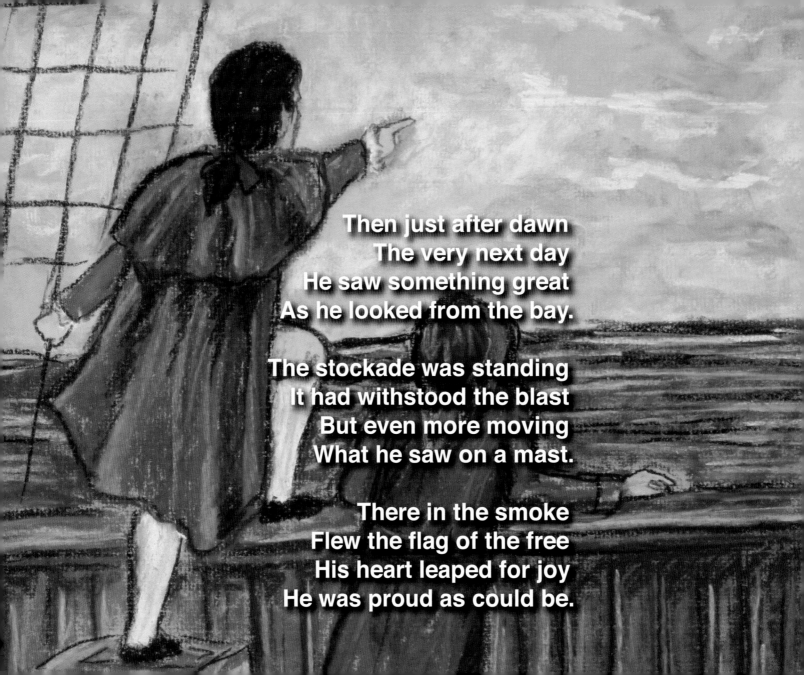

Then just after dawn
The very next day
He saw something great
As he looked from the bay.

The stockade was standing
It had withstood the blast
But even more moving
What he saw on a mast.

There in the smoke
Flew the flag of the free
His heart leaped for joy
He was proud as could be.

He saw stars and red stripes
From where he now stood
The battle was over
The outcome was good.

The flag was a symbol
That we wouldn't give in
Though the battle was hard
The fight we would win.

As Francis was taken
Back to the shore
His heart filled with pride
As never before.

He wrote down some words
As they popped in his head
Line after line
He liked what it said.

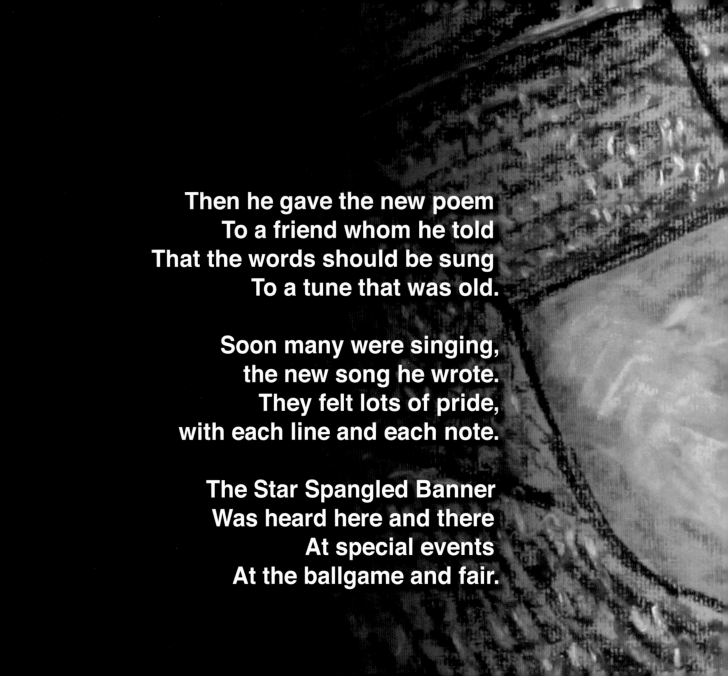

Then he gave the new poem
To a friend whom he told
That the words should be sung
To a tune that was old.

Soon many were singing,
the new song he wrote.
They felt lots of pride,
with each line and each note.

The Star Spangled Banner
Was heard here and there
At special events
At the ballgame and fair.

Then many years later
The Congress proclaimed
It's our National anthem
And called it by name.

Each time its now played
And each time we hear.
We solemnly stand
And sing loud, and cheer.

When the song Francis wrote
Rings out strong and clear
It stirs patriot hearts
With thoughts of what's dear.

Of our nation and freedom
Of great days gone by
And great things still coming
The limit - the sky.

This book is dedicated to Emma, my youngest granddaughter. She is a "one of a kind jewel." She constantly reminds me that this nation is built upon the principle that each of us have value in our unique individualism. The importance of the individual is at the heart of why this nation holds such an important place in the history of mankind.

## Acknowledgements

Kayee's illustrations are remarkable – she has such a gift. Kirk Hawkins deserves special thanks for his tireless work in designing the book so that it flows and so that the verse and illustrations can be enjoyed to their fullest. His creative insight is awesome (Thanks, Lisa for bringing him into our lives.)

*Timothy Penland*

ISBN: 978-1-93565-101-7

Library of Congress Control Number: 2010923112

Illustrations by Kayee Au
Cover and Interior Design by Kirk Hawkins

Printed in India

1 2 3 4 5 6 7 8 / 14 13 12 11 10